Pre-History to Mother's Day, 1985:
The world over, mothers tell their children things like "Don't run with a lollipop in your mouth" and "Always wear clean underwear in case you have an accident."

Mother's Day, 1985:
Michele Slung and Ballantine Books publish MOMILIES®, the first book to collect and celebrate all those wonderful, worrisome, witty, and wise sayings.

Mother's Day, 1985 to Mother's Day, 1986:
From all over America, Ms. Slung receives letters—from people eager to share their own momilies!

Mother's Day, 1986:
MORE MOMILIES® is published—an all-new collection sure to delight moms and kids of all ages.

More Momilies®

As My Mother Used to Say...®

MICHELE SLUNG

BALLANTINE BOOKS • NEW YORK

Library of Congress Catalog Card Number: 86-91098

ISBN 0-345-33493-0

Manufactured in the United States of America

First Edition: May 1986

For My Father,
who, by marrying
my mother, made
all my momilies
possible

Rafael Slung

Author's Note

The idea for the book that became *MOMILIES®: As My Mother Used to Say®*, had its origins in my passion for making lists. Thinking one day of that particular phrase which my own mother had produced on so many occasions (when I seemed to be taking an overinflated view of myself)— "You're not the only pebble on the beach" was what she'd say, ominously—led me to wonder how many other of her familiar utterances I could call to mind.

Not so surprisingly, it wasn't difficult to come up with more, once I cast my ear back to my childhood: "Always clean up in the kitchen as you go along." "You can't tell what it looks like until you try it on." "You don't have to *like* them; they're your relatives." "Put some color in your cheeks." "The more you scratch it, the more it's going to itch."

The list grew longer and longer. And once I started with my own, I began to be curious whether everyone else possessed equally unforgettable maternal maxims. So I started asking friends and the friends of friends. To my delight, practically all of them quickly emerged as zealous "momily" recollectors! Postcards came in the mail;

there were momily messages on my answering machine. And I became a connoisseur of the especially eccentric or useful ones.

When someone turned out to be a bit uncertain just what a "momily" was, I'd say simply, "It's anything your mother told you that you've never forgotten." No matter what kind of wisdom or wackiness the momily contains, my definition of it also holds that if it still zings into your mind on the proper occasion, if you can still hear your mom's tender (or sarcastic, or hectoring) voice, then what you've got is the genuine article.

This book, *MORE MOMILIES®: As My Mother Used to Say®*, is the result of new friends and readers—people across North America, from Shreveport to Saskatchewan, even across the Pacific, from Hartford to Honolulu—enthusiastically sharing their "momilies" with me. Having put a name to the phenomenon (phe-*mom*-enon?), I heard from men and women both old and young, from the children of Irish, Italian, Swedish, Dutch, Greek, French, Hungarian—you name the nationality or religion!—mothers. It didn't take long for me to see just how "momilies" were a sort of universal language.

Naturally, I'd suspected this must be so—after all, how many times was I told "Everyone has a mom?"—but it was truly wonderful, even downright exciting, to have it proved so conclusively, over and over again.

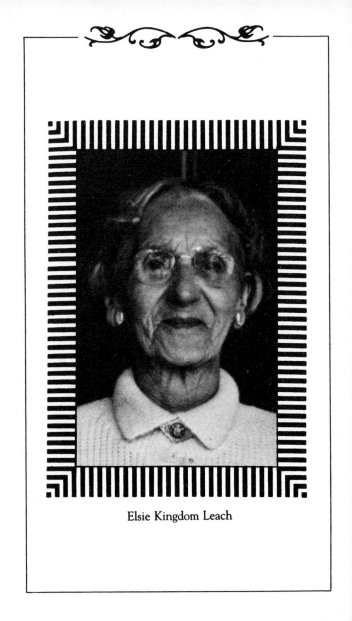

Elsie Kingdom Leach

"If I've Told You Once..."

Don't get smart with me.

Don't be a pill.

That's not a face I'd advise you to make too often.

Don't raise your eyes to heaven. God won't help you.

I'm not talking to you for my health.

Look at me when I'm talking to you.

Julie Löwy Kafka

What I say goes in one ear and out the other.

Don't mumble. I graduated from mumbling school.

Didn't you know I've got eyes in the back of my head?

Do I look like a short-order cook?

I've only got one pair of hands.

You kids can fight. But you can't bite and scratch.

No matter *what* you're playing with, you can poke your eye out with it.

3

Don't ever put anything in your ear except your elbow.

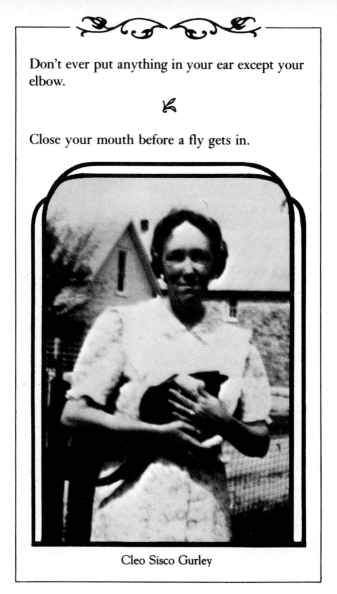

Close your mouth before a fly gets in.

Cleo Sisco Gurley

Don't bang the screen door!

Don't stand there dripping on the floor!

Stick your head back in the window! Do you want to lose it?

You're going to break your neck!

If you fall out of that tree and break your leg, don't come running to me.

Why? Because "y" is a crooked letter.

Just because.

"Hey!" is for horses.

"Wait" broke the bridge.

Sarah Glantz Berlinger

Too much laughing leads to crying.

You children would try the patience of an iron saint.

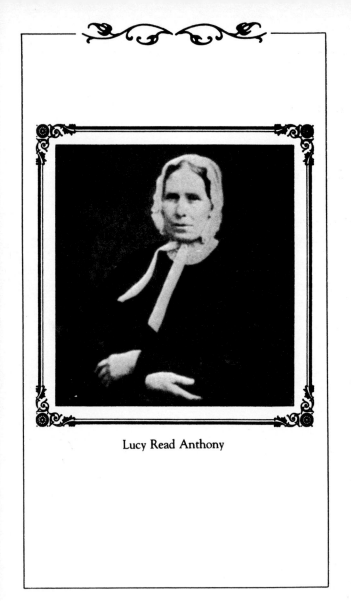

Lucy Read Anthony

What Are Mothers For?

Fool me once—
  Shame on you!
Fool me twice—
  Shame on me!

Do you think I got these bumps on my head from falling off a turnip?

I was your age once.

I could just eat you up.

Every child in America is born to be president.

Irena Spenser Pym

I'll forgive and I'll forget, but I'll remember.

I wouldn't give you a nickel for another one, but I wouldn't take a million for the ones I've got.

I've done my best. An angel could do no better.

Remember, I'm your mother—and you'll never have another.

Mothers know everything, except for things that change.

My mother didn't leave me anything of value except her wisdom.

Every day is children's day.

Bernice Layne Brown

Mom Sharpens Her Tongue

If I wanted to know your opinion, I'd ask for it.

&

I'm *not* everyone else's mom.

&

I've heard *that* one before.

Everything you're thinking about, I've already done.

Mary Litogot Ford

Pretty is as pretty does, and you're pretty apt to stay that way.

❧

You'd lose your head if it weren't tied on.

❧

What did you do? Leave your brains at school?

❧

If brains were dynamite, you wouldn't have enough to blow your nose.

❧

You'd go to the ocean and not find any water.

❧

Don't stand there grinning like a wave on a slop bucket.

So *who's* happy? Cows in the field are happy.

If you're born to hang, you won't drown.

Nell Carter Yule

Don't be stupid, stupid.

Try to pretend you're normal.

You call *that* a kiss?

Ida Stover Eisenhower

Setting an Example

Why can't you be more like your brother [sister]?

❧

It never hurts to be polite.

❧

You can at least pretend to have a good time.

❧

A lady doesn't keep people waiting.

Never ask personal questions.

Little children should be seen and not heard.

Lena Bogardus Phillips Lardner

Whistling's for loafers.

Whistle before breakfast; cry before noon.

An empty can makes the most noise; the same goes for heads.

Don't talk with your mouth full.

You only have so many words in your voice box.

People spend too much time talking from their teeth out.

The tongue, the tongue—we spend three years learning how to use it and the rest of our lives learning how to control it.

If there's a silence, it's your fault.

Share your toys.

Jane Lampton Clemens

Good enough isn't good enough.

Good, better, best—
    Don't let it rest.
Until the good gets better,—
    And the better best.

God's work is done. Have you done *your* part?

Never do anything you wouldn't want to see
published in your hometown paper.

What will the neighbors think?

What would Jesus say?

Evangeline Lodge Land Lindbergh

Mom Predicts

The day you're born is the day you draw your last peaceful breath.

You'll understand when you're older.

You'll get over it before you're married.

Wait until you grow a mustache.

Maybe in a year or two...

Grace Caroline Swanson Hefner

When they're little, they step on your toes.
When they're grown, they step on your
heart.

You'll thank me someday.

You'll be sorry when I'm six feet under.

Lucetta Todhunter Stout

Well, It Could Happen

Don't point—you'll get warts.

Don't sing at the table—you'll get a crazy wife.

Eat your beets so your cheeks will be pink.

Don't eat standing up—you'll get fat legs.

৯

Burnt bread makes you pretty.

Ann Geilus Austerlitz

If you sew on a Sunday, you'll have to rip out all the stitches with your nose on Judgment Day.

Don't sit on the table, or you'll never get married.

If you wear hand-me-down shoes, you're stepping into someone else's problems.

Don't go around with one shoe on, or one of your parents will die.

Step on a crack; break your mother's back.

What falls on the floor arrives at the door:
a fork—a gawk
a knife—a wife
a spoon—a loon.

If your right palm itches, you're going to get money. If your left palm itches, you'll be in a fight.

Mollie McQuillan Fitzgerald

Kiss your sister good night even if you're mad at her. You don't know if you'll see her in the morning.

If you pout like that, a chicken's going to come and sit on your lip.

Amy Otis Earhart

"This Hurts Me More Than It Hurts You"

If you don't stop crying, I'll give you something to cry about.

If you don't stop that, I'm going to slap the black off of you.

If you don't watch out, I'll hang you by your toes.

I intend to spank you within an inch of your life.

If you can't behave, you're going to be eating off the mantelpiece.

Ann Snyder Boothe

Believe me, if you can't listen, you can feel.

Ɣ

That's just a taste of what you'll get next time.

ⱨ

Better you shed the tears than me.

Ɣ

I've killed kids for less than that.

ⱨ

If you don't think I mean it, just try me.

Ɣ

It's a lot hotter where you're going.

ⱨ

Wait till your father gets home.

Edwina Dakin Williams

Take This to Heart

If it isn't yours, you don't want it.

When in doubt, say no.

Save your good times till later.

Don't we have enough trouble without borrowing it?

It's nice to be important but more important to be nice.

Always tell the truth, even if you have to lie to do so.

Susan Phillips Lovecraft

I can forget and you can forget, but a piece of paper never forgets.

What you don't have in your head, you have to have in your heels.

When your mind doesn't work, your feet have to.

If you want something done—go. If you don't—send.

Always be aware of the consequences.

Always expect the worst, and when it comes, make the best of it.

Don't dig a foundation where you don't plan to build a house.

Don't take a single thing for granted—ever.

Frances Allethea Murray Smith

Never lower yourself to act like the opposition.

If they don't want to play with you, then you don't want to play with them.

It's not so important what happens to you in life as how you deal with what happens.

Try not to associate with anyone you can't learn something from.

Life is what you make it.

Jean Harlow Carpenter

Birds and Bees, Boys and Girls

If you bite your nails, it shows you're boy-crazy.

Go out with him—you don't know who you'll meet.

Don't let that boy spend too much money on you.

Treat all girls as if they were your sister.

Gladys Smith Presley

For every Jack, there is a Jill.

Where cobwebs grow,
there comes no beau.

All men are the same. They just have different faces so you can tell them apart.

You'd better marry a man who'll give you a personal maid.

No girl you marry is going to pick up after you.

If you stoop to marry, you'll never get up.

Don't make yourself too available.

Don't cheapen yourself.

Mayann Armstrong

Never advertise what you don't have for sale.

Petting is for animals.

No man chases a streetcar he's already caught.

Constance Bicknell Auden

"Don't Play With Your Food!"

Stop pushing your food around on the plate.

Ɂ

You eat what's put in front of you.

Ɂ

Your eyes are bigger than your stomach.

Ɂ

Never eat tuna fish at a drugstore.

Eating ice will give you a stomach ache.

Don't eat the last inch of a cucumber—it's poisonous.

Myra Edith Cutler Keaton

Always pull off the strings on a banana—they give you a stomach ache.

Liverwurst is something you eat ten minutes before you die.

An orange is gold in the morning, silver at noon, and lead at night.

Eating celery is good for the nervous system.

As soon as you can count twelve bubbles, turn the pancakes.

Only take a little on the first helping.

Don't make a pig of yourself.

Janet Woodrow Wilson

Always eat three square meals a day.

Always order from the middle of the menu.

Don't eat in front of your friends unless you have enough to share.

Meat is tougher where there's none.

Frances Roche Shand-Kydd

"Do You Want Me to Call the Doctor?"

You've only got one body, and you'd better take good care of it.

Don't smoke—it'll stunt your growth.

A cigarette has a fire on one end and a fool on the other.

If you wear galoshes inside, you'll get a headache.

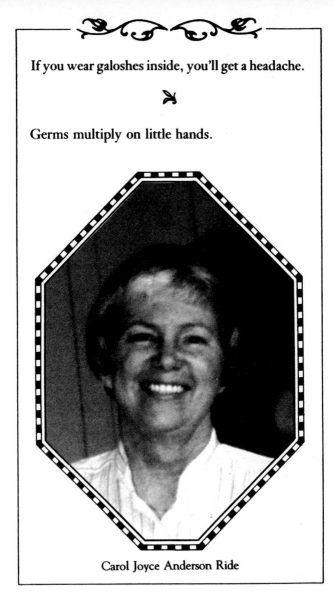

Germs multiply on little hands.

Carol Joyce Anderson Ride

Always take the cotton out of the pill bottle—it collects germs.

Don't crack your knuckles—you'll get arthritis.

Don't sit on the cold ground—you'll get galloping consumption.

Don't go outside with wet hair—you'll get pneumonia.

A little fresh air wouldn't kill you.

Remember, you can get sunburned on a cloudy day.

The important thing is to drink plenty of fluids.

Janet Lee Bouvier Auchincloss

Practically Speaking

How you behave at home is how you'll behave outside the house.

If you're bored, why don't you pick up your room?

Time to change your clothes and put your apron on.

Never leave the kitchen empty-handed.

Elzire Legros Dionne

If you make a mess, you're going to have to clean it up.

🍂

If I let you get a dog [cat, bird, fish, hamster, etc.], I'll be the one who winds up feeding it.

🍃

Fish and company smell after three days.

🍂

Don't stand there with the refrigerator door open—everything will defrost.

🍃

Turn out the lights. We don't own stock in the electric company.

🍂

We don't *own* the Edison—we *owe* it.

Flowers should always look "happy" in a vase.

If you leave things behind at other people's houses, you'll never be invited back.

Jana Semanska Navratilova

Never give a purse without putting money in it.

Always look down the chute a second time whenever you put a letter in the mailbox.

Make a reservation. You can always cancel it.

Gloria Morgan Vanderbilt

The Tried and True

How do you know you don't like it if you haven't tried it?

❧

Don't throw out dirty water until you have clean.

❧

It's always the weeds that grow the best.

❧

What goes around comes around.

Sorry doesn't mend it.

Manners maketh man.

Emily Norcross Dickinson

One step at a time is all it takes to get there.

What's past hope is past grief.

There's a place for everything and everything in its place.

Things done by halves are never done right.

A quitter never wins and a winner never quits.

You're only as old as you feel.

Don't cut off your nose to spite your face.

Look it up—you'll remember it longer.

Anna Rachel Berman Asimov

Big Mom Is
Watching You

You're not going out like *that*, are you?

Stop frowning—you'll be old before you're thirty.

Remember to smile—it's an improvement.

Don't you think people look at the back of your hair, too?

Your hair's not clean till it squeaks.

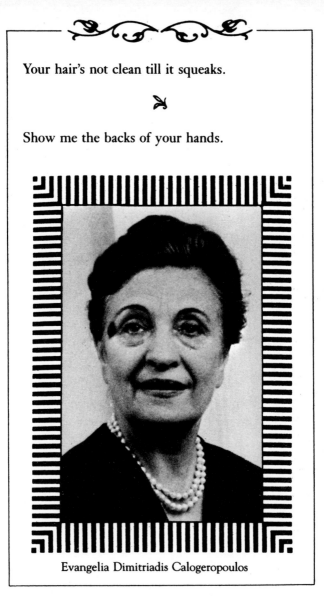

Show me the backs of your hands.

Evangelia Dimitriadis Calogeropoulos

Do your nails really taste *that* good?

X Y Z—Examine Your Zipper.

KYLC—Keep Your Legs Crossed.

And this time make sure you use soap!

Fanny Schneider Mailer

The Dress Question

Put on your sweater—I'm cold.

🌿

Are you sure you're warm enough?

🌿

Always wear a white collar. It brightens your face.

🌿

Never wear red, or you'll be taken for a hussy.

Earrings that dangle are not for daytime.

It doesn't matter what you wear on a Friday.

Kate Adams Keller

Wearing hats make you go bald.

Always take a bath before putting on clean underwear.

Gentlemen are known by their heels.

Don't ever go outside wearing slippers.

No matter how poor you are, wear expensive shoes.

It's ... okay. But you can find something nicer.

Cheap is cheap.

Eliza Grace Symonds Bell

Mom Gets Folksy

Promises are like pie crusts—they're made to be broken.

If you're scared of the dark, remember the Ark.

I'll show you how the cow ate the cabbage.

Only the spoon that stirs the pot knows its troubles.

If wishes were pots and pans, there wouldn't be any tinners.

𝕶

When you look at your feet, your feathers fall.

Ada Mae Wilkey Day

Still waters run deep, but the devil's at the bottom.

Ƹ

There *is* a devil, there is no doubt.
—But is he trying to get inside of us or out?

Ƹ

Cleft in the chin,
—Devil within.

Ƹ

The devil has many tools, and the lie is the handle that fits them all.

Ƹ

"It won't be long now," said the monkey with his tail cut off.

Ƹ

As you slide down the banister of life, don't get a splinter in your career.

If you burn your tail, you're going to have to sit on the blister.

Flora Amelia Rivé Leonard

Two wrongs don't make a right, but two Wrights made an airplane.

What's poured over the horse's back will meet under his belly.

Don't spit up in the air—it'll fall on your nose.

Don't swallow the bull and leave the tail hanging out.

It'll never be noticed on a galloping horse.

Mary Walsh James

Acknowledgments

Again, I'd like to thank all the friends, friends of friends, mothers of friends, and friends who are mothers—not to mention the kind readers and radio and TV audiences—who shared "more momilies" with me: Elkan Abramowitz, Juliet Annan, Ronald Ball, Jack Bogat, Joe Brown, Karen Budirsky, Nancy Coffey, Barbara Cohen, Jack Cole, Robert (Chip) Cunningham, Judy-Lynn del Rey, Herb Denton, Connie Drummer, Berry Dyson, the Flynn family, Lynn Goldberg, Robert Goldstein, Liza Graham, Karen Gundersheimer, Russ Gould, Jana Harris, Barbara Howson, Susan Isaacs, Mary Jarrett, Leslie Kobylinski, Mrs. Paul C. Lyles, Robert Masello, Marilyn McCallum, Inez McClintock, John Meyers, Olivia Miles, Charlene Parker, Marcy Posner, Jody Powell, Bonnie Prudden, Eden Rafshoon, Laurie Rovtar, Lorraine Shanley, David Snyder, Susan Stamberg, Faith Stone, Jane Stubbs, Ednamae Storti, Margaret Ward, Sister Agnes Clare Warren, Liz Williams, Dan Yergin, Susan Zises.

Special thanks, too, go to: Stuart Applebaum, Robert Harrell, Edward Mendelson, Sylvia Morris, and Mark Ricci.

KEY TO PHOTOGRAPHS

page father of:

v   Michele Slung

page mother of:

x   Cary Grant
2   Franz Kafka
4   Helen Gurley Brown (*Helen Gurley Brown*)
6   Milton Berle (*Memory Shop*)
8   Susan B. Anthony
10   Barbara Pym (*Hilary Walton*)
12   Edmund G. "Jerry" Brown (*California State Library*)
14   Henry Ford (*From the Collections of Henry Ford Museum and Greenfield Village*)
16   Mickey Rooney (*Memory Shop*)
18   Dwight D. Eisenhower (*Dwight D. Eisenhower Library*)
20   Ring Lardner (*Ring Lardner, Jr.*)
22   Mark Twain (*Mark Twain Project, The Bancroft Library*)
24   Charles Lindbergh (*Marceauphoto, Minnesota Historical Society*)
26   Hugh Hefner (*David Hefner*)
28   Rex Stout (*John J. McAleer*)
30   Fred Astaire (*Memory Shop*)
32   F. Scott Fitzgerald (*Matthew Bruccoli*)
34   Amelia Earhart (*Schlesinger Library, Radcliffe College*)
36   Clare Boothe Luce (*Clare Boothe Luce*)
38   Tennessee Williams (*Photography Collection, Harry Ransom Humanities Research Center, University of Texas at Austin, TX*)
40   H. P. Lovecraft (*H. P. Lovecraft Estate*)
42   Rosalynn Carter (*Rosalynn Carter*)
44   Jean Harlow (*Memory Shop*)
46   Elvis Presley (*Graceland*)
48   Louis Armstrong (*Frank Driggs Collection*)
50   W.H. Auden (*Berg Collection, New York Public Library*)
52   Buster Keaton (*Museum of Modern Art, Film Stills Archive*)
54   Woodrow Wilson (*Woodrow Wilson Collection, Princeton University Library*)